Matter Splatter!

Contents

Features

Matter matters. The word *matter* is a homonym. Find out more about homonyms on page 5.

Read about the man who split the world's smallest particle into even smaller pieces in **Splitting the Atom** on page 7.

Why would people take to the water in cardboard boats? Read **Cardboard Creations** on page 24 to find out.

You can have a lot of fun experimenting with matter. Try **Balloon Blowup** on page 28 and see what you can learn.

How are matter and energy connected?

Visit www.rigbyinfoquest.com

for more about ENERGY.

What's the Matter?

From the clothes we wear to the milk we drink, everything in the universe is made of matter. If it takes up space, or has any **mass,** it is matter. Some matter, such as the homes we live in, is easy to see. Other matter, such as the air in a balloon, is **invisible.** Some matter, such as steam from a kettle, seems to be here one moment and gone the next.

Most matter can be found in one of three forms called states. Matter such as wood is solid. Matter such as water is in a liquid state. The air we breathe is a gas.

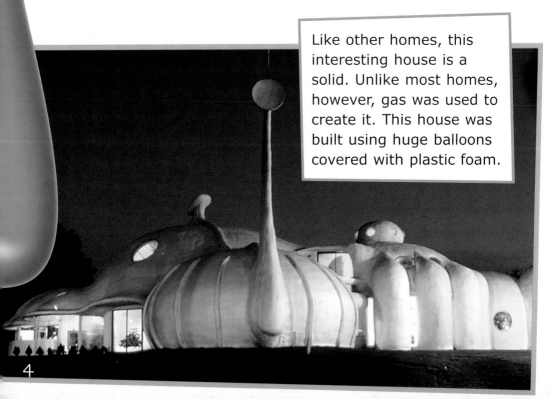

Like other homes, this interesting house is a solid. Unlike most homes, however, gas was used to create it. This house was built using huge balloons covered with plastic foam.

The word *matter* is a homonym. Homonyms are words that are spelled the same and sound the same but have different meanings. *Matter* can mean "material" or it can mean "to be important." How many other homonyms can you find in this book?

Solid

Liquid

Gas

Milk is a liquid. Cow's milk is made up of about 88% water, but unlike water, it contains almost all the nutrients that people need for good health.

5

All matter is made up of invisible particles called **atoms.** Sometimes these atoms join together to make **molecules.** In solid matter, atoms and molecules are packed closely together. They are not easy to break apart. Atoms and molecules in liquids are not as tightly packed. This is why we can pour liquids. In gases, the atoms and molecules are very loose so they can move around easily.

These water molecules are loosely packed. The escaping molecules are even looser. They show water, a liquid, **evaporating** into steam, a gas.

PROFILE

Splitting the Atom

Ernest Rutherford (1871–1937)

Electrons travel around the center of an atom, called the nucleus.

Ernest Rutherford was a scientist from New Zealand who made a discovery that changed science and the way we think about the world. For many years, scientists thought atoms were the smallest particles in the universe. Then, in the early 1900s, Ernest Rutherford discovered that an atom contains tiny negatively charged particles called electrons.

Later, Ernest Rutherford became the first person to break up the nucleus of an atom. This led to the important development of nuclear power.

A nuclear power plant

7

States of Matter

Solid Stuff

It is difficult to think of life without solids. Can you imagine walking around without being on solid ground? Thankfully, most solids are hard, but an object does not have to be hard to be a solid. It may be hard or soft, heavy or light. All solids have one thing in common—they keep their shape.

Pressure needs to be applied to solids to break them. Some solids, such as pencil lead, need only a little pressure before they break. Other solids, such as concrete, need a lot of pressure. Every year, people throw away billions of tons of solid garbage. Discarded solids such as metal and plastic damage the environment.

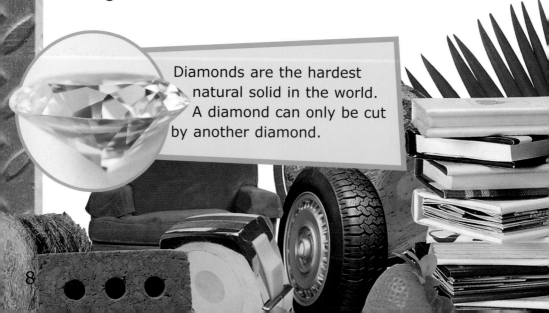

Diamonds are the hardest natural solid in the world. A diamond can only be cut by another diamond.

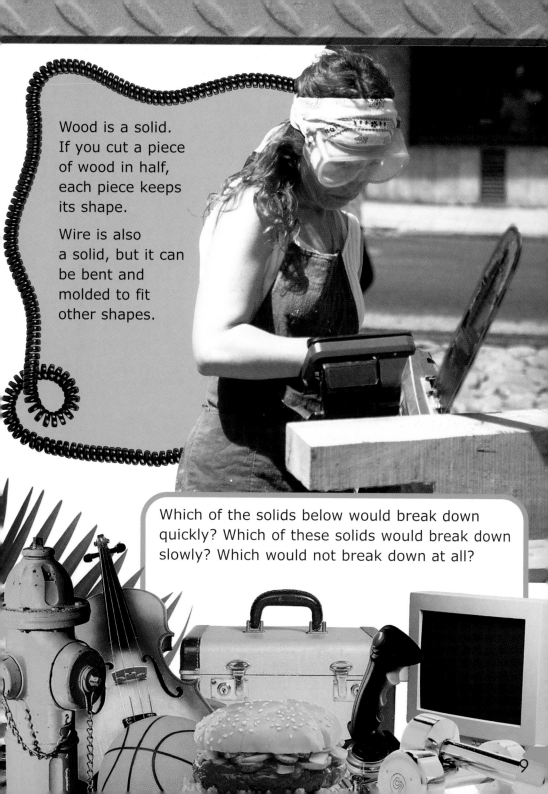

Wood is a solid. If you cut a piece of wood in half, each piece keeps its shape.

Wire is also a solid, but it can be bent and molded to fit other shapes.

Which of the solids below would break down quickly? Which of these solids would break down slowly? Which would not break down at all?

Lovely Liquid

We all think of ourselves as being quite solid. Humans are, in fact, made up mainly of liquid. The molecules in liquids are not fixed to each other in any particular way, so liquids do not have their own shapes. They always take the shapes of their containers. This is lucky for us. It means our blood can travel to every part of our body.

The most important liquid on Earth is water. It is easy to forget all the ways we use it. We drink it, wash in it, swim in it, and play in it. Water is also vital to plant growth and in the manufacturing of many items.

Did you know that glass isn't a solid? It is actually a liquid! It is so **viscous** that it takes centuries to flow. If you had the tools to carefully measure a very old window, you could prove it. You would find the bottom of the glass would be slightly thicker than the top.

Some liquids do not stay liquid for long. Liquid concrete must be kept moving or it will dry into a solid. Concrete mixers with rotating drums keep the liquid moving until it is ready to be poured out and shaped.

11

It's a Gas

Gases are all around us, even
though we can't usually see them.
Gases do not keep their shapes. We may
be able to contain them in a tire or a balloon,
but once released, gases move in all directions.
Most gases have two very useful properties.
They can be **compressed** and they can **expand**.

Like solids and liquids, gases have mass. Gases are
thinner and lighter than solids and liquids, however.
Helium is a very light gas. It is even lighter than air.
It is sometimes used in balloons.

Some gases are **flammable**. Different flammable
gases can be used to power many things from
lawnmowers to spacecraft.

Air, which is a gas, is lighter than water. That is why inflatable toys are able to float on water.

WORD BUILDER

During the 1600s, scientists realized that some matter can exist in a state similar to air. They wanted the name for this state to describe the way air can fill any amount of space. So they invented the word *gas* by changing the Greek word *chaos*, which means "space."

13

Time for a Change

What Causes Change?

Everything in the universe is continually changing. Nothing remains the same. Change in matter is caused by energy. Heat energy causes molecules to speed up. If enough heat is used, some solids can become liquids, and some liquids can change to gases.

Movement energy can also cause matter to change. The Grand Canyon was formed by the movement of the Colorado River running through it. Nature itself is one of the greatest changers of matter. All matter that was once alive **decomposes.** When matter is broken down, it releases nutrients. Nutrients are very important to the growth of living things.

Huge amounts of heat energy are needed to make molten, or hot liquid, glass. The ingredients melt together at 2,600—2,900°F.

Over millions of years, the movement of the Colorado River eroded many layers of rock, creating a canyon 1 mile deep and 277 miles long.

SITESEEING · SCIENCE & TECHNOLOGY ·

How are matter and energy connected?

Visit www.rigbyinfoquest.com
for more about ENERGY.

How Matter Changes

Matter changes in two very different ways. Some changes are only temporary. Water can be frozen to form ice and then warmed to form water again. Some changes, however, are permanent. When a log of wood is burned, it creates ashes. No matter how hard you try, the ashes can never be changed back into wood.

Some changes take a very long time. Over millions of years, matter from plants and animals decays and is pressed together. This matter eventually changes into coal or oil. Some changes, however, are sudden. Earthquakes, volcanoes, and flash floods can greatly alter the landscape in minutes.

Ice is one of the most unusual solids in nature. The solid form of most substances is heavier than the liquid form, but this is not true of ice. A volume of ice weighs less than the same volume of water.

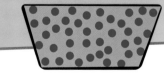

At 60°F, water fills this bowl. The water molecules move about freely.

Coal was formed from the remains of plants that died one million to four million years ago. After millions of years of compression, the plant matter turned into coal. While the plants lived, they stored up energy from the sun. This energy remains in the coal. As the coal is burned, it produces energy in the form of heat.

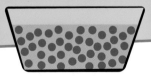

At 39°F, the water contracts and fills only part of the bowl. The molecules move closer together.

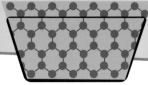

At 32°F, the water freezes into solid ice and expands. The molecules move apart and form a rigid pattern of crystals.

Putting It Together

Mixtures and Solutions

We use the terms solid, liquid, and gas to describe matter because they are easy to understand. Most things, however, are mixtures. Your favorite soda may be a mixture of solid sugar, liquid water, and carbon dioxide gas. Some mixtures are called solutions. Solutions are created when a solid is dissolved in a liquid. Sea water is a solution. It contains a large amount of dissolved salt.

Often mixtures and solutions can be separated into their various states. Salt can be removed from the sea by evaporation. Pressure can be applied to olives to get olive oil.

What Is a Bubble?

Most of us know that bubbles are not solid, but are they liquid or gas? The answer is they are both! A bubble is a thin sphere, or ball, of liquid with air or other gas inside.

Olives are a mixture of oil, which is a liquid, and fruit pulp, which is a solid. Olive oil is used in cooking.

1 Whole olives are 10–40% oil.

2 Pressing machines are used to squeeze the oil out of the fruit.

3 The oil is separated from the fruit pulp.

4 The oil is bottled and sold.

Awesome Alloys

An alloy is a special kind of mixture. An alloy is formed when different metals are melted and then mixed together. The new metal formed is usually quite different from the metals used to make it.

Over 5,000 years ago, people found that if they combined copper and tin, they created a much stronger metal. This new metal was called bronze.

One of the most widely used alloys is steel. Steel is made from iron, carbon, and manganese, and it's known for strength and durability. One of the early problems with steel was that it rusted. Scientists found that by adding nickel and chromium, they could create a new rustproof metal. Because of this discovery, we now have stainless steel.

Soda cans are often made from aluminum alloys which are strong and light.

Different types of steel can be used for structural beams, frames to support cranes and other heavy machinery, aircraft landing gear, and bicycle frames.

Did you know that certain spiders can produce silk that is five times as strong as steel? Some companies are seriously looking at finding ways to produce enough spider silk for use in the building industry.

Some scientists believe that closely woven spider silk would be the ideal material for bulletproof vests!

21

New Materials

Fantastic Plastic

Plastics, or **polymers**, are very special types of matter. They are not found naturally in the environment. Plastics are created by changing the molecules found in oil. The discovery of plastics has made modern life much easier. Plastics have replaced many natural materials in products. In many cases, we can now use plastics instead of wood, paper, glass, and some metals.

Plastics are very useful, but they do have a harmful side. Plastics do not easily break down, and discarded plastics are becoming an environmental problem.

Plastics are lightweight and do not rust or dent easily. This makes them perfect for artificial limbs and joints.

Plastic products are made from plastic **resins.** The resins melt into a syrupy liquid when heated.

Blow molding is used to make hollow plastic objects such as bottles. Blow molding uses air or steam to expand a tube of molten resin, forcing the material against the walls of a mold.

Plastics can be shaped into almost any form. Plastics can be as rigid as steel, as soft as cotton, or rubbery and waterproof.

Cool Cardboard

One of the main advantages of cardboard over plastic and metal is that it is less harmful to the environment. Cardboard is made from recycled paper. This breaks down quickly. Cardboard is used in packaging everything from furniture to fruit drinks.

That is only the beginning. At Westborough School in England, an entire school building has been made of cardboard. It includes an after-school club, locker rooms, kitchen, and washrooms. Cardboard tubes have even been used to support the roof!

IN THE NEWS

August 5

Cardboard Creations

More than 1,500 people took part in the annual Great Cardboard Boat Regatta on Saturday.

The first challenge for those taking part was to design and build a human-powered boat from cardboard.

The second challenge was to complete three trips around a 200-yard course. For those not used to either boating or the bendable nature of cardboard, this was a little tricky. Race day proved to be a soggy day for some competitors, but a fun day for all!

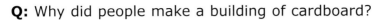

Q: Why did people make a building of cardboard?

A: Because cardboard is made from recycled paper and can be recycled, too, so it is a "green" material. Cardboard is also a cheap building material. Thirdly, it was fun to try out new ideas.

Q: Is the building waterproof?

A: Cardboard is not waterproof, so the outside of the building was covered with a mixture of wood pulp and cement. This also made the building stronger and fire resistant.

Inside the cardboard club

Outside the cardboard club

Sticky Stuff

Adhesives, which we normally call glues, are truly amazing. Many years ago, glue was made from animal and plant parts. It didn't smell very nice! It also didn't work nearly as well as modern adhesives. Some of today's adhesives can support the weight of a 10-ton truck without coming unstuck.

Adhesives are used for a wide range of purposes. We think of cars as being mostly metal. There are actually over 20 pounds of adhesives in an average car. Adhesives are even used in space. Over 30,000 heat resistant tiles are glued onto each NASA space shuttle.

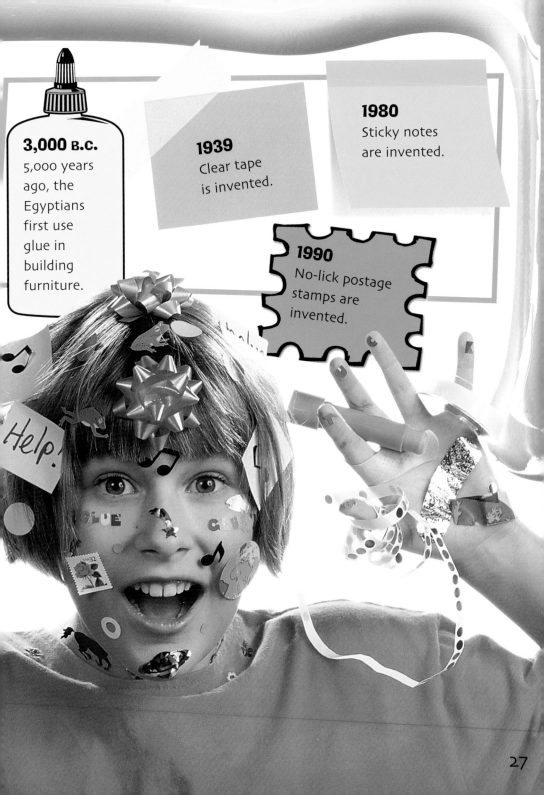

3,000 B.C.
5,000 years ago, the Egyptians first use glue in building furniture.

1939
Clear tape is invented.

1980
Sticky notes are invented.

1990
No-lick postage stamps are invented.

27

Balloon Blowup

TRY THIS!

You will need:
- a balloon
- a small funnel
- a spoon
- baking soda
- a plastic bottle
- vinegar

VINEGAR

BAKING SODA

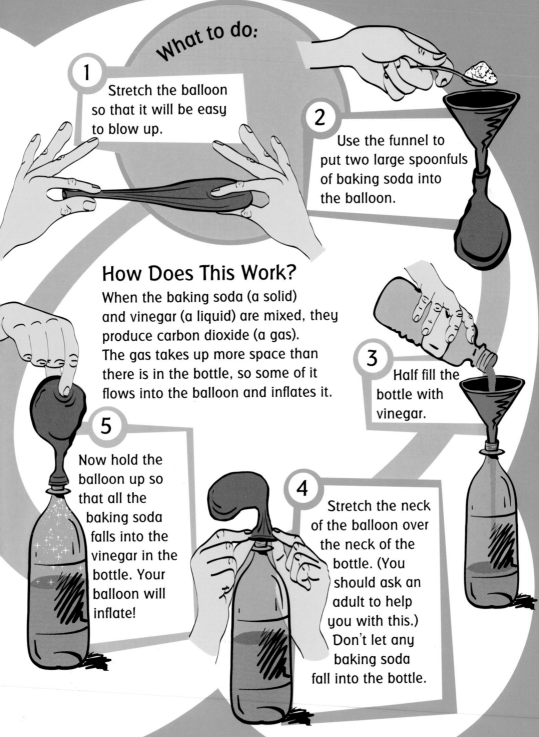

What to do:

1 Stretch the balloon so that it will be easy to blow up.

2 Use the funnel to put two large spoonfuls of baking soda into the balloon.

How Does This Work?

When the baking soda (a solid) and vinegar (a liquid) are mixed, they produce carbon dioxide (a gas). The gas takes up more space than there is in the bottle, so some of it flows into the balloon and inflates it.

3 Half fill the bottle with vinegar.

4 Stretch the neck of the balloon over the neck of the bottle. (You should ask an adult to help you with this.) Don't let any baking soda fall into the bottle.

5 Now hold the balloon up so that all the baking soda falls into the vinegar in the bottle. Your balloon will inflate!

29

Glossary

atom – one of the tiny particles of which all things are made

compress – to force something into a smaller space. When gas is compressed, it pushes against the sides of its container. This is how a bicycle tire is inflated.

decompose – to rot or decay

evaporate – to change from a liquid into a gas

expand – to grow larger. When gas is heated, it expands and takes up a larger amount of space. This is how a hot-air balloon is inflated.

flammable – easily set on fire

invisible – unable to be seen

mass – the weight of matter

molecule – two or more atoms joined together. A water molecule is made of two hydrogen atoms and one oxygen atom.

polymer – a large molecule formed by the joining of at least five smaller molecules

resin – a polymer used as the basis of plastics, adhesives, and varnishes. Resin makers often add pigments to color the resin and reinforcements such as glass fibers to give plastics extra strength.

viscous – being thick and sticky. A viscous liquid is so thick it is almost a solid.

Index

Research Starters

1 Squishy matter can be fun. Can you find a recipe to make your own slime? What experiments could you do with slime?

2 You have learned that a diamond is the hardest natural solid in the world, but what matter is a diamond? Find out more about diamonds and how they are formed.

3 Fun things can be made out of cardboard. What cool things made from cardboard can you create?

4 Cooking often involves matter changing from one state to another. Use a simple recipe to make a flow diagram describing the changes that the matter makes at each stage.